If you have ever wondered—or even if you have never thought about it at all—what mysteries the Sphinx and the Great Pyramid hold for you and your soul's initiation on the path of enlightenment, you will discover in this original work by Etelka Holt how you can apply the ancient wisdom in your life today. God has entrusted the sacred mysteries to his prophets, messengers, and servants that his children might have the opportunity for greater self-knowledge and self-mastery. This book will provide the key to unlock the door to the Great Pyramid of Life that is your Real Self.

the
Sphinx
and the
Great Pyramid

the
Sphinx
and the
Great Pyramid

A Record in Stone
of Man's Attainment
of the Christ Consciousness

Etelka Holt

Summit University Press
Los Angeles

The Sphinx and the Great Pyramid
Published by
THE SUMMIT LIGHTHOUSE
for Church Universal and Triumphant
Box A
Colorado Springs, Colorado 80901

LIBRARY OF CONGRESS CATALOG CARD NUMBER: 77-75735

INTERNATIONAL STANDARD BOOK NUMBER: 0-916766-25-X

Printed in the United States of America

Summit University Press
Third Printing

ACKNOWLEDGMENT

To the Messengers of The Summit Lighthouse and their Staff, without whose encouragement and assistance I would have been unable to share my belief that the Ancient Wisdom was brought from Atlantis to the Sphinx in Egypt to await an awakening world. The views expressed in this book are not intended to be a reflection of the Ascended Masters, the Messengers or their teachings.

God has blessed your undertaking. He has shined upon it. He has released the light of freedom. So he has sent forth a blessing for the raising-up of the Pyramid of Life within your heart. Stone by stone, let the pyramid be built—not as an outer symbol or an outer sign—but let the pyramid be within your heart a holy shrine. Let it be dedicated now to the ascension of every man, woman, and child upon this earth.

—Saint Germain

PREFACE

Periodically, there are items in newspapers extolling the wonders of the tomb of Pharaoh Khufu. Friends visit the Great Pyramid and knowing my interest bring me guide books and even today these books inform the visitor that the pyramid is nothing but a tomb. In 1968 a guide was closely questioned, he assured my friend there was nothing, absolutely nothing, to the idea of the relationship of this great structure to the Bible.

My interest in the Great Pyramid was inspired in 1941 during my professorship at Kansas State College in Pittsburg, Kansas. One of my students drove sixty miles twice a week to attend a series of lectures given by a minister who believed the pyramid to house a divine revelation. His enthusiasm has become mine and my library of pyramidology has expanded through the years.

Study of the works of such pyramidologists as David Davidson, Howard B. Rand, Adam Rutherford, Peter Tompkins and Pat Flanagan along with information given by Edgar Cayce, and knowing as we all do that the end of the Age is but some thirty years away gave a feeling of urgency to prepare a short "story" of the Great Pyramid that is not a **tomb**. Much of the material of this treatise has been used in church groups and by men and women of no particular creed or religion who had a sincere desire to know more about the structure and the Master Architect.

It is my hope that it will make you want to expand your reading and study of the Bible and will increase your interest in and appreciation of this book, the Bible. So for the present put aside your preconceived ideas and be willing to read that which to many may seem fantastic.

As man evolves spiritually the existence and use of the cosmic forces will be revealed to him. Since my publication of this treatise, a number of books by learned men from many parts of the world have been written. Most of the writers agree that the Pyramid corroborates the Bible narrative. However, I have yet to find one which deals with this vast information as the cosmic knowledge from Lemuria and Atlantis which with the fall of Atlantis was brought to Egypt for preservation.

It is with the hope that if you read this book you, too, will be enthused with the wonders of this knowledge which today is so rapidly beginning to be understood by many. With this hope this book is revised.

Etelka Holt

September 3, 1968
December 1, 1975

It has been proved that the Great Pyramid is not a tomb. It will be shown in the following thesis that mathematicians and astronomers have demonstrated beyond a doubt that by measurements it does confirm the Bible story which is a guide to man's spiritual evolution. The chronograph of the Great Pyramid revealed the correct dates of events in ancient history long before the event took place. Thus, if that which was predicted occurred, does man have the right to limit the Power that built these great monuments by refuting the prophecies concerning the next centuries?

Because of the perversion of the God conciousness to the human ego, destruction of Atlantis seemed inevitable; consequently, vital information which had been gained there was hidden in a small pyramid, sometimes referred to as the Pyramid of Records, between and connected with the Sphinx and the Great Pyramid. The Cayce Readings revealed that within this Hall of Records are prophecies concerning the last half of the 20th century and the records of the "People of One God from the beginning of man's entrance into the Earth." It is the consensus that these records are to be available when the world is ready to receive and interpret them and utilize the information. If this knowledge were to be brought into the open today, the condition could be much the same as in Alexandria when misguided and malicious individuals in the early centuries of the Christian Era destroyed priceless books and tablets.

In addition to these records which may in the future be made available to a regenerated world, the Great Pyramid itself serves as a timetable of the span of human experiences recorded in the Bible and a further assurance that God's word is true and will not fail us while we experience the coming events it sets forth.

STOREHOUSES OF KNOWLEDGE

To Preserve the Ancient Wisdom

THE SPHINX! One of the oldest stone monuments in the world. THE GREAT PYRAMID! The only one of the Seven Wonders of the Ancient World still standing.

Interested? Of course you are, whether you are (1) one of those who believes the Great Pyramid is only another of those many pyramids in Egypt used for tombs; or (2) one who believes that by measurements and symbology it confirms the Bible story; or (3) one who believes these great structures of stone were built to preserve the vast knowledge of man's spiritual evolution well-known in Atlantis; or (4) one who believes they have a special spiritual-scientific significance, particularly for this age.

Both the Great Pyramid and the Sphinx are believed to have been built to preserve the ancient wisdom brought from Atlantis to Egypt. Since the information given to the world by Edgar Cayce in the last decade, we have had a much clearer idea of the reason for the construction of these historic stone monuments and of the date they were built.

And now I have told you before it came to pass, that when it is come to pass, ye might believe. John 14:29

ILLUSTRATIONS

CONTENTS

ix

ONE HUNDRED TWENTY- FIVE
CENTURIES AGO

The Sphinx is Built

Across the Nile from Cairo on the Gizeh Plateau
stand the Sphinx and the Great Pyramid. The Sphinx,
facing eastward and lying some 480' southeast of the
Great Pyramid, is carved out of the solid rock on which it
rests. A composite of bull, lion, eagle, and man forms
this figure in stone. Although dwarfed by its neighboring
monuments, this immense figure is 189' long; the
manface is more than 16' high. Through thousands of
years as the Sphinx stood guard over the entrance to the
Pyramid of Records, it has periodically been covered up
to its neck in sand and as many times excavated. A huge
granite stela between the forepaws tells that it was once
uncovered as the result of the dream experienced by
Tuthmosis IV. The Sphinx as a god bade him release his
suffocating body. To this day the ever encroaching sand
strives to envelop this ancient symbol which antedates
the Pyramid by many years.

Each individual has his place in God's great plan for mankind, but on Atlantis many had "fallen" from fulfilling their part. Highly developed individuals saw the destruction that would come to the world and knew that the story of God's design for the evolvement of humanity needed to be preserved for the generations to come.

The Great Pyramid

There is a vast difference of opinion as to when the Great Pyramid was built. This is probably because the human mind cannot conceive of any man-made structure standing thousands of years. Historians and students agree that it was built more than 4,500 years ago. But within the last ten years research of the Edgar Cayce Readings has been made which gives the date of building as 10,449-10,349 B.C. and gives the story of the predicted sinking of Atlantis as the reason for the transfer of priceless material from Atlantis to Egypt for safekeeping.

The Great Pyramid was planned as a record in stone which would last through thousands of years until man had reached a plane of spiritual evolvement that would enable him to see and interpret the message. It was imperative that the site for the Great Pyramid furnish as stable a foundation as possible because of the esoteric knowledge it was to house. The point chosen was higher than any of the land that was inundated by flood and, too, it was near the center of the Earth land masses which made it less vulnerable to earthquakes. The geographical location of the point where the base diagonals intersect is latitude 29° 58' 51" north; longitude 31° 09' east.

Without doubt the building itself merits all the appellations by which it has been designated: Mountain of Stone, Pillar of Stone unto the Lord of Hosts, Witness That Corroborates the Bible, One of the Seven Wonders of the Ancient World, Metrological or Geometrical Expressions of Divine Revelation, God's Word in Stone, and Edgar Cayce's reference to it as "a record in stone of the history and development of man."

The sides of its thirteen and one half acre base form a perfect square approximately 760', and each is oriented north, south, east and west, showing an error of only five seconds. On a four-sided pyramid-shaped structure, there should be an apex or capstone. But the base circuit of this Pyramid was purposely made less than the designed base circuit by 286.1 pyramid inches, hence the Apex Pyramidion could not be placed at its proper height. This displacement symbolizes man's self-willed displacement from God and his rejection of the truth — the falling short of the human race. The Displacement Factor has proved to be the cosmic theme of Pyramid revelation.

The sides of the Pyramid are equilateral triangles which slant inward coming together at the top in such a way that the apex would have been 481' perpendicular to the base diagonal. It is a marvel of engineering skill, and the accuracy of construction parallels a watchmaker's precision.

Cayce relates that a covering composed of "an alloy of copper, brass and gold" was pounded into shape for the top of the Pyramid, and when it was placed there was an elaborate ceremony of dedication. At certain times of the year a cosmic fire was lighted on top of the Pyramid in a manner known only to the Atlanteans. This metal top was desecrated by order of the Pharaoh under whom the children of Israel were slaves.

There are approximately 2,300,000 individual stones in the "Pillar," each averaging two to two and one-half tons, including some weighing as much as 54 tons. The limestone came from the Mokkatam Hills about 12 miles distant and the granite from 500 miles to the south. So perfectly are the stones cut that where they are laid side by side a thin point of a sharp knife blade will not penetrate between them. The builders had a knowledge of materials: granite which expands and contracts with heat and cold was used in the inside construction, while the limestone used on the outside becomes harder and more marblelike in appearance when exposed to the weather. The whole was hermetically sealed including the door opening. Before the highly polished white casing stones were torn off, the Pyramid must have accurately portrayed the "Lights and Measures," as it was called in some of the records. The glistening white limestone reflected the sun's rays, providing an enormous sundial visible for many miles. Job could have been referring to it when he spoke of "a molten looking glass." (Job 37:18) These casing stones are nearly all gone; some may be seen in buildings in Cairo and some lie buried in the sand nearby. The Pyramid itself is of solid stone masonry, except for the passages and two good-sized chambers, and has a mass comprising 90 million cubic feet. Subterranean chambers and passageways were cut through the solid rock of the plateau on which the Pyramid stands. (Illustration I.)

It has been proved that the builders understood mathematics and astronomy. Through a system of number symbology it is revealed that they knew the dimensions of Earth and its orbit, the number of days in the solar year, the Precession of the Equinoxes, and the law of gravitation. They were aware of the relationship of the diameter of a circle to its circumference and considered "pi" important enough to incorporate it in the "revelation."

Considered from a purely materialistic viewpoint, the knowledge displayed by these builders makes it quite certain that no ordinary human being could have produced a design "so basically simple and yet manifesting such a profound knowledge of the 'science of creation'." Edgar Cayce verifies what these thoughts indicate: the Great Pyramid was built "by the application of those universal laws and forces of nature which cause iron to float. By the same laws, gravity may be overcome, or neutralized, and stones made to float in air. The Pyramid was built by levitation."

THE SPIRITUAL SIGNIFICANCE
OF THE PYRAMID BEGINS TO COME
INTO CONSCIOUSNESS

The True Significance of the Pyramid Takes Form

No little importance can be attached to the fact that the interior was kept hidden for more than 11,000 years and that at an opportune moment the sound of a falling stone inside the Pyramid spurred an Arab chief's workers on to the discovery of the passages. Calif Al Mamoun had set men to tunneling into this so-called tomb in search of treasure. They were about to give up when the sound came to them from a short distance. With renewed efforts they reached a downward passage. Following this passage, they came to the place where the fallen stone revealed an ascending passage blocked by a granite plug. Tunneling around the obstruction they searched the ascending passages and finding neither gold nor jewels they abandoned the interior. Could this not be a manifestation of a Higher Power? It was another thousand years and more until the Great Pyramid began to give up its secret to men who were ready to hear the Voice.

In the years 1638, 1763, 1799, and 1837 men from England and France explored the interior of this great structure and made valuable contributions concerning the various passageways and their distinguishing features. In 1799 three French scientists made trigonometrical surveys and accurately measured its base.

In 1859 John Taylor, scientific instrument maker of London, studied, researched and published the results of his work. He concluded that the ratio of the height to the base circuit was as the radius of a circle is to its circumference and that its builders were familiar with pi or 3.1416. Mr. Taylor advanced the hypothesis that the Pyramid was built to convey a divine revelation, and that its unit of measure was the Polar Diameter inch. He held that the world possessed a building of inspiration — the Great Pyramid — as it had long possessed a book of inspiration — the Bible.

Five years later C. Piazzi Smyth, Astronomer Royal of Scotland, made detailed surveys of the exterior measurements embodying dimensions and motions of earth and its orbit. He agreed with Taylor on all points. In 1865 Mr. Smyth received a letter from Robert Menzies of Leith who suggested that the Pyramid represented God's plan of redemption and outlined what the various passages meant to him. For a while there was great interest in this and there began a study of the measurements, but a few years later intellectualism squelched this new idea.

Within the next decade Sir Flinders Petrie confirmed Smyth's measurements but *utterly rejected any divine idea in the building*. He said it was built as a tomb. Because of his standing in intellectual circles he received the patronage of the Royal Society and even today his views are the views of orthodox universities and colleges and encyclopedias. Its spiritual message has been ignored by the majority of the people. Perhaps the very fact that for so many years it was thought to be a tomb has kept its spiritual message intact until the time when man must be made aware of the validity of Bible prophecy.

Between the years 1925 and 1955 David Davidson, a structural engineer and mathematician of great ability began his study of the Pyramid to uphold Petrie's theory that it was built as a tomb. He was an agnostic and began his work to prove that any claims to its divine origin were false. He was to become the outstanding expert in Pyramidology of modern times. By 1929 he admitted that the Bible and the Pyramid were related. He said he never claimed to have been led by God, but that many times he was "compelled by God" even against his own will and interest to find solutions which are now becoming available for study. He proved to his satisfaction that the Pyramid was a God-given revelation for a scientific age — a perfect example of precision in accuracy of detail and construction.

Mr. Davidson was the first to establish the Pyramid's prophetic chronology on a scientific foundation and work out the Displacement Factor. Before his death he said, "I proclaim in humility and yet with confidence that the Great Pyramid's message establishes the Bible as the inspired word of God."

Displacement One Key to the Revelation

Man is made in the image of God; thus he has the potential of God's perfection. But man by free will falls far short of this state. The Displacement Factor of the Great Pyramid symbolizes mankind's rejection of divine guidance and is consistently illustrated physically, historically, and spiritually throughout the passages, chambers, and the platform whereon the Apex Pyramidion was to have been placed.

Examples of the Displacement Factor, 286.1", are (a) base circuit was 286.1" less than the designed circuit, (b) center of all passages, ascending, descending, and horizontal, has been placed 286.1" to the east of the North-South axis line. The King's Chamber is the first place where Displacement can be overcome. This chamber has been designated as the Chamber of the Mystery of the Open Tomb. Whatever its name, it signifies that the risen Christ is here to help mankind; for humanity is free to cross the Open Tomb, symbolizing the overcoming of death.

While displacement has not been overcome for mankind as a whole, it may be said that from time to time certain individuals have been restored to spiritual understanding as evidenced by the many ascended masters. The Capstone is the emblem of the Christ or God-power which Jesus manifested in such measure that he could heal the sick and raise the dead. As the wayshower to humanity he told mankind that they too could utilize this power. The placement of this headstone would mean that the Christ conciousness had been established within each one, individually and collectively, and that man, now fully enlightened, had realized his divine purpose and could stand with the lamb on Mt. Zion.

Number Symbology

Designs of God's creation are perfect. Numbers play a significant role in the wondrous pattern of God's Word and works. The books of the Bible reveal the secrets of God in numbers: days are numbered, answers to how long and how many are given in numbers. The prophesies are set forth in numbers. The activities of man are governed by numbers — hours of days, days of years. Designs of nature are dependent on number — a certain number of leaves on a stem, a certain number of kernels of grain in a head.

The Teleois proportions used throughout the Pyramid are 1, 4, 7, 13, 19, 25, 31 and based on three-line dimensions record knowledge past and future. They are basic in the Universe and form the highest spiritual concept of numerology.

David Davidson's dates and proportions, using one-line measurements, give the computations he made based on the geometry of the solar year, 365.2422 days.

Within the passages and chambers is found the Pyramid's chronograph.

The Time Line Includes the Millennium

What is referred to as the Time Line is an arbitrary line agreed upon by scholars in an effort to explain the written history of mankind as recorded in the Bible. It extends from approximately 4,000 B.C. (the date for the time of Adam) to 2,000 A.D., the beginning of the millennium as given in the Book of Revelation, (Rev. 20: 3-7), and extending one thousand years from 2,000 to 3,000 A.D., the end of the millennium when all evil will have been eliminated and planet Earth will be ready to ascend.

INTERPRETATION OF THE DIVINE PLAN
OF PASSAGEWAYS

Passageways Numbered for Convenience

A study of the passageways and chambers of the Great Pyramid not only helps to explain the Bible story, but gives the history and development of man from Atlantean times to the end of the millennium, 3,000 A.D. The records are written in different kinds and colors of stone used in construction and by means of mathematics and astronomy in a manner far too profound and transcendent for the ingenuity of man to devise. Among other ways, changes are indicated by scored lines on some passages, by layers and types of stone, and the direction in which the turns of the passageways are made.

A Descending Passage

The numbers following correspond with those on Illustration I.

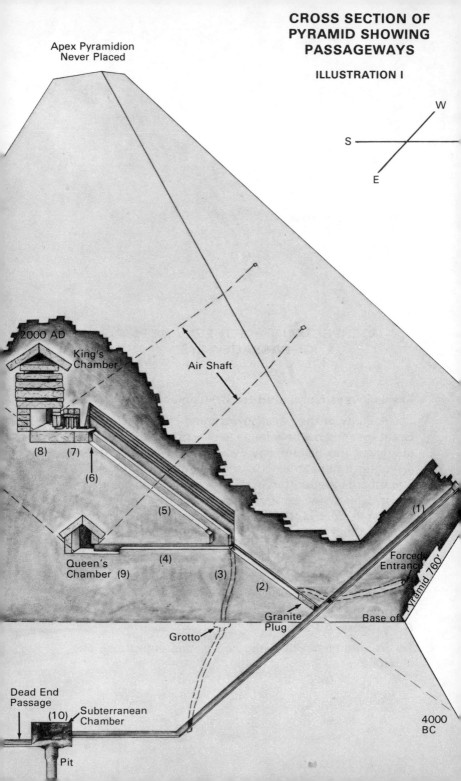

CROSS SECTION OF PYRAMID SHOWING PASSAGEWAYS

ILLUSTRATION I

Apex Pyramidion Never Placed

W
S
E

2000 AD

King's Chamber

Air Shaft

(8) (7)

(6)

(5)

(1)

Forced Entrance

(4)

Queen's Chamber (9)

(3)

(2)

Granite Plug

Base of

Pyramid 760'

Grotto

Dead End Passage

(10)

Subterranean Chamber

Pit

4000 BC

(1) The entrance to the Pyramid which is 50" above the base and 286.1" east of center, was so cleverly concealed that it was not discovered until the Arab Calif's workmen found it from the inside. Today's Pyramid visitors use the forced entrance which is somewhat nearer the ground level. From the original entrance the passage slopes downward signifying spiritual degradation as the result of the departure from perfection. It leads to the Subterranean Chamber, the Pit, and the Dead End Passage.

The Ascending Passage

(2) A granite plug 206.666" long (width of King's Chamber) concealed the entrance to the Ascending Passage, and the knowledge contained in the chambers above was accessible only by the guidance of a Higher Power. In point of time the entrance to the Ascending Passage signifies the Exodus.

The Well and the Grotto

(3) The low ascending corridor changes abruptly into a much higher passage and here part of the floor is torn away to reveal the openings to two low passages, one horizontal, the other descending. To the right is an extremely steep descending shaft known as the Well which widens into a room called the Grotto. The Well signifies Jesus' three-day experience in the sepulcher proving life to be deathless. Though man sinks to a low estate there is hope for him in the power of the Christ consciousness to return to the Light of God.

Entrance to the Queen's Chamber

(4) Directly ahead and beneath the floor of the Great Hall is to be found the entrance to the Queen's Chamber. This will be discussed under the material on the Queen's Chamber to be found on page 32.

The Grand Gallery

(5) The Grand Gallery represents the Christian Era when life took on new meaning. In this passageway mankind can stand upright, for the Gallery is 28' high, 286.1" higher than the roof line of the first Ascending Passage. Built into this passage are the main symbols of the Christian Dispensation. Reducing the width of the corridor to 3½' are ramps nearly 2' high and 1¾' wide on either side of the passage. Into each are cut 28 miniature tombs. These graves are open — emblematical of the fact that as Jesus the Christ was raised from the dead by the glory of the Father, even so we also walk in newness of life through the Christ, our resurrection. The Bible pictures the Christian Dispensation made up of seven churches headed by seven stars which are the angels of the seven churches, (Rev. 1, 2). Seven courses of overlapping stone run the whole length of the Grand Gallery forming both sides. This is the Gallery of seven courses; it is seven times higher than the entrance passage.

Something of the magnificence of the Grand Gallery may be experienced from Illustration II. This shows the removal of part of the floor of the north end of the hall which made a gap in the inclined plane of the ascending corridor and revealed the two other passages, one on the right into the Well Shaft and the other directly ahead into the Queen's Chamber at the heart of the Pyramid. There is a 6' climb before progressing upward along the floor of the gallery. At the far end, symbolically, man can stand at the top of the Great Step, look back at the progress he has made and forward to the attainment of his spiritual fulfillment.

The Great Step

(6) Five feet before the outlet of the Gallery is the Great Step, 3' high, symbolizing the time when man

THE GRAND
GALLERY

ILLUSTRATION II

6'

To Queen's
Chamber

To Well
and Grotto

began a definite step forward. There was a great upsurge of industrialization, culture, learning, and religion, also it marked the beginning of the age of modern transport. As it was a time of extreme astronomic development, the symbolism of the Great Pyramid began to be understood.

Growth of human power without sufficient spiritual accompaniment was unconscious preparation for World War I.

Noah had 120 years of warning before the flood (Gen. 6:3, 11, 13 and Heb. 11:7) and the Gospel of Luke tells us "as it was in the days of Noah, so shall it be also in the days of the Son of man." (Luke 17:26)

The apex of the capstone if laid would have been directly over the junction of the North-South and East-West axis lines. The Great Step was in alignment with the East-West axis, but there was no way to get to the North-South axis line until humanity reached the King's Chamber.

Horizontal Passages: "The Boss"

(7) These passages, lead through (a) more Gallery or Altar Platform, (b) First Low Passage, (c) Antechamber, (d) Second Low Passage to the entrance to the (8) King's Chamber. The scale is now increased approximately 12 times. Each Pyramid inch indicates 30 days rather than a year as it did previously. (Illustration III).

Very early records give titles to some of the passageways that have a greater spiritual significance than the later names — Grand Gallery, Hall of Progress; The Great Step, The Great Uplift. The top of the Great Step where there is still five more feet of Gallery, now level, is called the Altar Platform of Etheric Consciousness because here one begins to understand the etheric nature of man and of the universe. Up to this period of history man lived in a world of solid matter, but now he has learned that matter is but energy vibrating at various rates of speed, that even the cells of his body are energy. With this understanding new ideas expanded rapidly and it is said that more than half of our present inventions came during those years.

The Altar Platform leads into a low 43" passage cut through limestone. It is called the Hall of Unity because unified action is necessary for success and progress.

From this low passage man emerges to the 12' Temple of Revelation, only to find it but 20" long; thus each individual is compelled to enter it alone. This Temple is unique in that its south wall is made up of the Granite Leaf, a heavy double sheet of granite wedged into the east and west walls to within 43" of the floor. It is really like a gate as it extends neither to the ceiling nor to the floor. On the north side of this leaf is a horseshoe-shaped stone, 5"x 5", exactly one Pyramid inch deep, indicating the units of measurement in the Pyramid and known as the "Boss".

The Hall of Adjustment is the 16" long space beneath the Granite Leaf and man must stoop to go under it.

The Chamber of the Triple Veil of which the Granite Leaf forms the north wall is again 12' high and is grooved on both sides, evidently prepared for other granite blocks. Directly in front, the stone of the south wall is cut so that it has the appearance of three tinted veils 9' long. The three grooves in the east and west walls of the Antechamber were built in such a way that three slabs could be dropped into place to form a triple door or portcullis to prevent entrance to the King's Chamber. In spiritual symbolism the doors were destroyed and the passing through the space or veil represents advancement toward illumination.

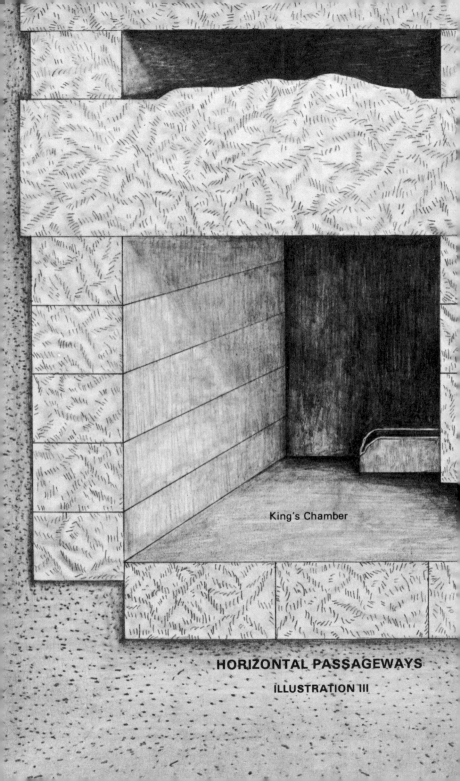

King's Chamber

HORIZONTAL PASSAGEWAYS

ILLUSTRATION III

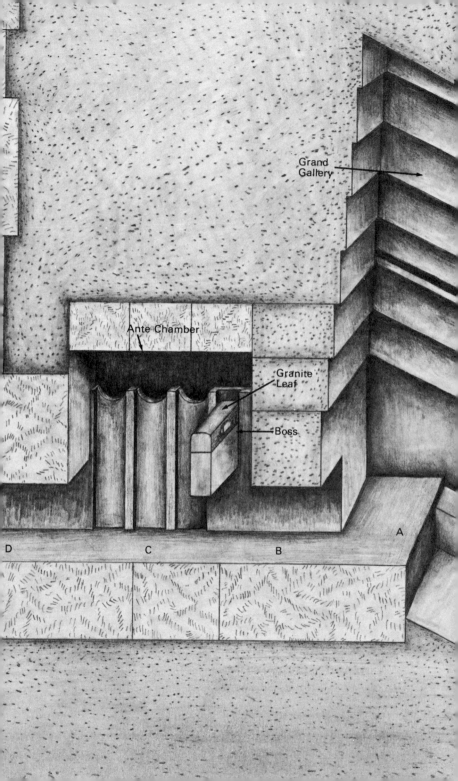

Grand
Gallery

Ante Chamber

Granite
Leaf

Boss

D

C

B

A

THE KING'S CHAMBER
REVEALS ITS SECRETS

First Place Where Displacement Can Be Overcome

This chamber is lined with five courses of equal depth of polished rose-pink granite signifying protection for God's chosen people. There are air vents some 3' above the level of the floor with shafts leading to openings in the north and south walls. Nine immense stone beams averaging 30 tons each comprise the ceiling and above are five chambers of construction designed to serve as a buffer from any violent shock.

The room is empty except for a lidless coffer cut from a single piece of brilliantly polished pink granite which lies 5' from the west, north, and south walls. This is not a sepulcher; no one was ever buried there. It is an open tomb and represents death swallowed up in victory — the resurrection.

Humanity Falls into Four Groups

According to the Time Line humanity reached the entrance to the King's Chamber September 16, 1936, (Illustration IV), and as they progressed the separation of mankind began according to their degree of spiritual evolvement. Humanity, whose goal is the ascension, naturally falls into four groups.

Each person may have the assistance of the ascended masters by making the call. The ascended masters are those souls who at one time or another have had the same life experiences as every man, but through obedience to the cosmic law and by their own free will have claimed the Christ consciousness or God-power.

1. Messengers: On reaching the King's Chamber this group makes rapid progress. They reach the middle of the west wall, turn east to cross the open tomb and for them death is overcome. Messengers are highly evolved spiritual beings in the plane of matter who have been appointed by the Masters to convey their sacred messages to humanity.

2. Watchmen and Builders: This group who may be said to be the "hundred and forty and four thousand" (Rev. 7:4), takes the most direct route, and as they approach the tomb, the Messengers advance to help them on their way.

So thou, O son of man, I have set thee a watchman unto the house of Israel; therefore thou shalt hear the word at my mouth, and warn them from me. (Ezek. 33:7)

. . . Watchman, what of the night? Watchman, what of the night? The watchman said, The morning cometh, and also the night . . . (Isa. 21:11, 12)

3. The Elect or Chosen People: These people make consistent progress but more slowly than the other groups. They may be said to be that great innumerable multitude of the Book of Revelation.

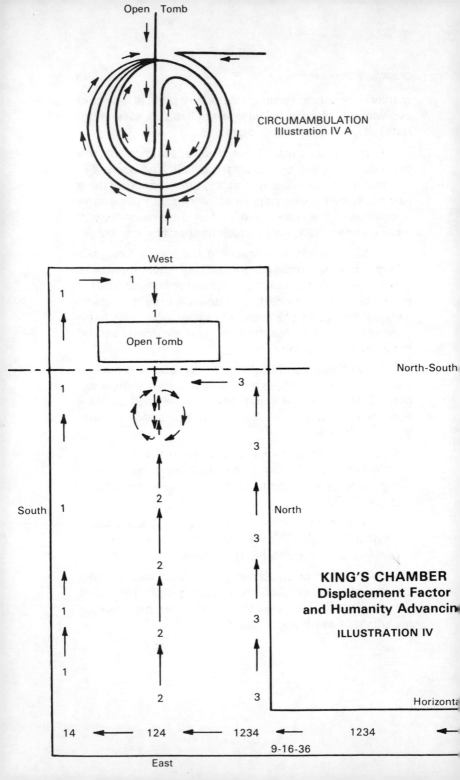

Open Tomb

CIRCUMAMBULATION
Illustration IV A

West

1

1

1

1

Open Tomb

North-South

1

3

1

3

South 1

2

North

3

2

3

1

2

3

1

KING'S CHAMBER
Displacement Factor
and Humanity Advancin

ILLUSTRATION IV

1

2

3

Horizonta

14

124

1234

1234

9-16-36

East

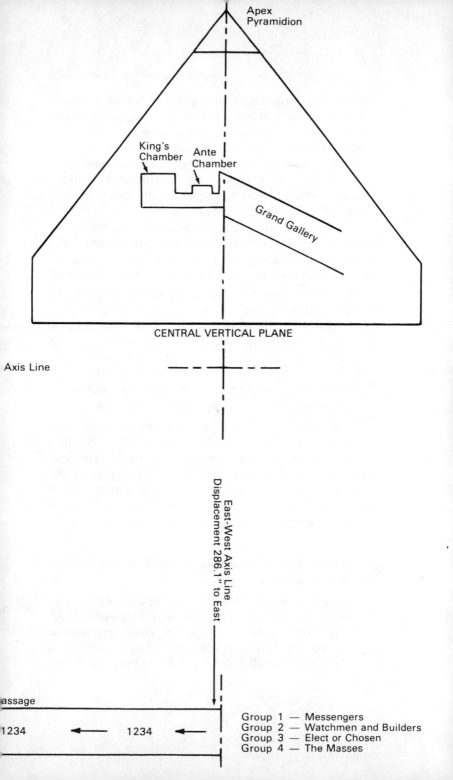

Apex
Pyramidion

King's
Chamber
Ante
Chamber

Grand Gallery

CENTRAL VERTICAL PLANE

Axis Line

East-West Axis Line
Displacement 286.1" to East

assage

1234 ← 1234 ←

Group 1 — Messengers
Group 2 — Watchmen and Builders
Group 3 — Elect or Chosen
Group 4 — The Masses

After this I beheld, and, lo, a great multitude, which no man could number, of all nations, and kindreds, and people, and tongues, stood before the throne, and before the Lamb, clothed with white robes, and palms in their hands; . . . Saying, Amen: Blessing, and glory, and wisdom, and thanksgiving, and honour, and power, and might, be unto our God for ever and ever. Amen. (Rev. 7; 9, 12)

Attitudes of the great innumerable multitude are changing and they are becoming more universally aware of the necessity of helping their less enlightened brothers that they too may become a part of the elect.

4. The Masses: These people come plodding along the east wall of the chamber looking neither to the right nor to the left, not even aware of the possibility of spiritual growth which the open tomb holds forth to everyone. When they reach the south wall some lose all hope for the future and many cease to care. The messengers and the watchmen have forever held out a helping hand to those masses who will accept it.

In July 1971 the Summit University was organized by Mark and Elizabeth Prophet of The Summit Lighthouse to stimulate the progress of all of the groups. It is cause for gratitude that many from among the masses, who previously had shown little interest, have also availed themselves of this opportunity to hear the sacred wisdom and make progress toward their ultimate goal.

Circumambulation Completes the Training for the First Three Groups

As each group reaches the open tomb, they carry on the ceremony of circumambulation. (Illustration IV A). Circumambulation is a mystical spiritual experience appreciated only by the spiritually minded. It has been a part of the ritual of all great religions of the past. Those taking part make a processional walk, usually three times, around the sacred object or the holy person, keeping the right side toward that which is encircled. As each man becomes aware of his individualized Christ consciousness, displacement is overcome for him. When the last of the three groups has reached the apex of spiritual evolvement, displacement will be sufficiently overcome for humanity that the capstone can be placed on the Great Pyramid.

The Open Tomb Symbolizes Death Overcome

Important in the allegory of the tomb is the cross of which the open coffer forms the central part. (Illustration V). At the close of his ministry Jesus revealed its meaning when he came forth from the sealed tomb. The

THE CROSS UNFOLDING

ILLUSTRATION V

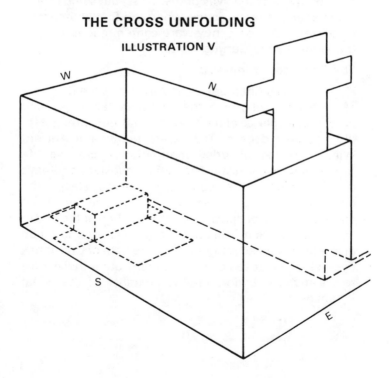

"Word of His Power" is shown symbolically by the cross unfolding from the open rock-cut tomb to stand at the ceiling level of the chamber representing a new order of man, one who avails himself of the Christ-power within him. It was necessary for Jesus to permit himself to be nailed to the cross that he might expose the powers of darkness rampant in the world which were ever on the move to overcome good. The true purpose of the cross is the freedom of humanity.

After the experience at Pentecost the followers of Jesus spread out over the country, and for a goodly number of years did outstanding healing work. There was no such thing as a church or an organized group. They simply called themselves The People of the Way or The Followers of the Way of the Cross; but some fifteen years after the resurrection when the first church was organized at Antioch, they were contemptuously called Christians by the Gentile world.

The Chamber of Initiation

The King's Chamber is also known as the Chamber of Initiation wherein the initiates after a long probationary period of training and trial were brought for their highest degree. They were taught the Ancient Wisdom which included mathematics, creative life forces, and cosmic laws. The initiation lasted three days during which time the applicant lay in a deep sleep in the open coffer; his spirit left his body to wander in the spiritual realms of space and return to him at the end of the appointed time. The initiate entered the tomb a man and returned an adept filled with the light of God. It has been said that Jesus as well as many other individuals received his initiation in this chamber of the Great Pyramid.

THE TWO WITNESSES

Pass the Word of God

The Hierarchical position of Christ for the Planetary body is assumed by a masculine and a feminine incarnation for every century in every age. To introduce the Aquarian Age the torch has been passed to Mark and Elizabeth Prophet who are the Two Witnesses for this century and part of their mission is passing the Word from God to man.

And I will give power unto my two witnesses, and they shall prophesy a thousand two hundred and threescore days, clothed in sackcloth. (Rev. 11:3)

Sackcloth is a symbol. In this instance it denotes that the witnesses come forth bearing their personal karma and, by the practical demonstration of the laws of cosmos, prove that every man and every woman can overcome his own karma by invocation to the sacred fires of the Holy Spirit. Some world teachers and all avatars have come forth as karma-free beings from birth. This means they balanced what karma they had, if any, in previous worlds. The advantage of having the witness "clothed in sackcloth" is to give hope to all that no matter how heavy their burden of past karma or the weight of sin, that so easily besets us and them, it can be made light by devotion to the Flame of the Holy Spirit and by service to God and man.

> And their dead bodies shall lie in the street of the great city . . . And after three days and an half the Spirit of life from God entered into them, and they stood upon their feet; and great fear fell upon them which saw them. (Rev. 11:8, 11)

This is not death as the world thinks of it, but a symbolic experience during the time when Groups 1 and 2 were making progress toward the open tomb — to overcome death. The experience began on August 20, 1953, during humanity's progress toward the tomb and ended July 23, 1972. This is being followed by a period of great awakening.

Significant Dates

July 23, 1972 — By this time Groups 1 and 2 are taking their part in reactivating the Mother Flame. No longer need we fear that evil will eventually triumph, because from this time on, all nations will be compelled to become subject to the administration of the Christ. It is significant that the conference held by our beloved Messengers, Mark and Elizabeth Prophet, when they carried the Flame to Ghana, Africa, ended on this date.

Autumnal Equinox, 1972 — Beloved Mark and Elizabeth Prophet, Messengers for the Ascended Masters, carried the resurrection flame to the Great Pyramid. (For detail see "The Cosmic Theme," page 36)

July 4, 1976 — Two hundred years after the signing of the Declaration of Independence indicates the exodus of subversives from the United States. The Christ number is 888. 1776 is twice that number.

October 31, 1976 — Group 3 has now crossed the open tomb and completed its period of circumambulation before the altar.

THE MILLENNIUM

Revealed in the Queen's Chamber

And now I have told you before it came to pass, that, when it is come to pass, ye might believe. (John 14:29) There are still two chambers to be considered — the Queen's and the Subterranean. These two have to do with the millennium, a time usually designated as between 2,000 and 3,000 A.D.

The Queen's Chamber

From the top of the low ascending passage the Queen's Chamber is reached by way of a low horizontal corridor directly beneath the inclined floor of the Grand Gallery. This passage is broken by one 21" step downward and leads to a room of limestone as compared to the granite of the King's Chamber. This corridor is a small scale duplicate of the Time Line from Adam to the beginning of the millennium. When the Queen's Chamber is reached, a blueprint copy of the millennium is revealed. (Illustration I, 9) The Chamber itself measures ten royal cubits, one cubit for each one hundred years of the thousand year period.

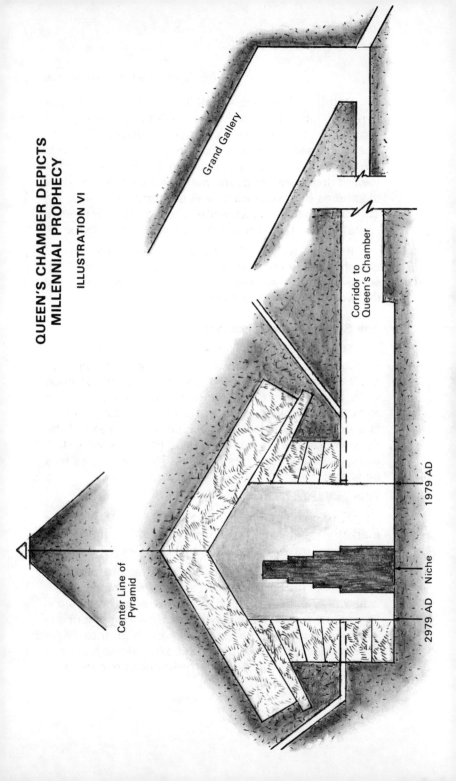

QUEEN'S CHAMBER DEPICTS
MILLENNIAL PROPHECY

ILLUSTRATION VI

Grand Gallery

Corridor to
Queen's Chamber

Center Line of
Pyramid

1979 AD

Niche

2979 AD

Within this room, which lies at the core of the Pyramid, (Illustration VI) is to be found a key to the proportions used in all the chambers and passageways. The time-space geometry indicated here is symbolic of the divine guidance man has had during his struggle toward displacement overcome. A series of seven sizes of spheres of increasing teleois proportions, 1, 4, 7, 10, 13, 19, 31 may be drawn within the walls of this room to reveal the sum of the divine period of the entire Pyramid.

It was by accident that the two air shafts leading into the chamber were discovered some time in the 19th century as they had only been cut to within five inches of the wall surface of the room.

The Subterranean Chamber

This chamber also is directly under the apex of the Pyramid and may be reached by way of both the well shaft and the descending entrance passage. (Illustration I, 10). In the floor of the chamber is a jagged hole referred to as the bottomless pit, large enough to endanger life. It is a deep cavity in natural rock below the base of the Pyramid. On the far side of the chamber is another low passageway which goes forward 54' and comes to a dead end.

Things Yet to Come

Autumnal Equinox, 1979-1994 A.D. — These dates mark the inauguration of the millennium as humanity in symbolism traverses the Queen's Chamber.

And I saw an angel come down from heaven, having the key of the bottomless pit and a great chain in his hand. And he laid hold on the dragon, that old serpent, which is the Devil, and Satan, and bound him a thousand years, And cast him into the bottomless pit, and shut him up, and set a seal upon him, that he should deceive the nations no more, till the thousand years should be fulfilled: and after that he must be loosed a little season. (Rev. 20; 1, 3)

Autumnal Equinox, 2979 A.D. — Humanity reaches the opposite side of the chamber. According to the Bible prophecy at the end of the millennium, Satan "must be loosed for a little season." He is released from the pit, but by this time the vibrations of good are so powerful that he only survives for "a little season."

Autumnal Equinox 2994 A.D. — The last date in Biblical and Pyramid prophecy marks the time when all death, misery — all evil — is removed from planet Earth which is now ready to rise into the higher consciousness.

THE COSMIC THEME

Progress Toward Christ Consciousness

On the cosmic screen of the Sphinx and the Great Pyramid can be read the story of the distant past and far into the future, although the time line of the Pyramid records only 7,000 years from 4,000 B.C. to 3,000 A.D. This is the end of the millennium as portrayed in the 22nd chapter of the Book of Revelation when all death and misery — all evil — will be no more and planet Earth and her evolutions will be ready to rise into the higher consciousness of the Christ, and the Feminine Ray will be restored to its rightful place in both man and woman. Our universe, including Earth, has been in existence many, many millions of years, but the 7,000 years depicted in the Pyramid is typical of progress both before and after that era, and reveals amazing knowledge of a small group of humanity who lived on Earth more than fifty thousand years ago and had retained a close relationship with the creative process.

With the submergence of Lemuria and much of Atlantis and with the warning that the rest of Atlantis

(Poseidon) would soon be under water, dedicated individuals realized the necessity of the preservation of the vast storehouse of knowledge that was theirs on Atlantis. Consequently, devout lifestreams carried the flame of knowledge to the land now known as Egypt. The Great Pyramid eventually became the repository for this treasure and for centuries, at least one hundred and twenty-five, it has been preserved and is only now beginning to be brought into the open for the eyes of mankind to see and to ponder. Knowledge on Atlantis was so advanced that our most learned scholars today would not entirely understand. This type of knowledge is what we shall expect to receive as the Pyramid unfolds its secrets.

After centuries of research by men from many different countries, it was agreed that the Pyramid did predict and point out not only the Bible story but the history of mankind's advance in the world. Within the last year or so, the Pyramid is being discerned as a storehouse of vast cosmic knowledge; for example, the source of bio-cosmic energy. In recent books concerning this storehouse, writers are beginning to point out new facts gleaned from comprehensive studies of the Pyramid; and as research continues and understanding increases, bit by bit the wisdom will be unfolded.

There has been much speculation in recent years about the type and source of energy used on Atlantis and Lemuria. Some researchers believe it could be the same energy which was generated by certain geometric shapes. Most geometric forms focalize energy which has an effect on living organisms. Brewers in Germany have long known that beer would not mature properly in square or angular containers. Only round shapes, such as bowls, would work. A pyramid, however, particularly one constructed in the proportions of the Great Pyramid, focuses an intense flame one-third of the way up from the base at the center of the pyramid. In the Great Pyramid of Gizeh, this is the location of the King's Chamber. This chamber is the first place where displacement could be overcome.

The very word "pyramid" denotes its great significance. In the Greek, the word **pyra** means fire or light or illumination that reveals something or makes things visible in the darkness. Number is the basis of the revelation, and **midos** means measure. The form of the Great Pyramid is said to represent the ascending resurrection flame soaring upwards towards its origin — a symbol of the spark of eternal Life returning to the sun of the universe. The ancient Egyptians spoke of the Great Pyramid as the Glorious Light; the Hindus called it the Golden Mountain; Strabo said, "It seemed like a building let down from heaven."

Mark and Elizabeth Prophet, Messengers for the Ascended Masters, together with a group of Keepers of the Flame, carried the resurrection flame from Colorado Springs to Egypt and on to the Great Pyramid. This was at the time of the autumnal equinox in 1972 and gave impetus to the approaching millennium. During the course of this visit, nine young men and one young woman climbed the Pyramid to see for themselves the size and condition of the place where the unfinished capstone would eventually be placed and to plant therein an immortelle, a flower that has been immortalized by the resurrection flame.

At 4 a.m. a full moon on the western horizon in Aries provided the only light for the first four barefoot men, clothed in Arab costume, to begin their ascent of the Great Pyramid of Gizeh. Each man climbed in the middle of the side assigned to him — north, south, east, and west. As they ascended they made calls for the raising of the four lower bodies of mankind. The four sides of the Pyramid represent the four cosmic principles of creation of which man's lower bodies are composed — fire, air, water, and earth. Through the evolution of the soul, these four lower bodies are to become one and so interwoven that man will no longer be conscious of his outer identity as separate from God, but he will recognize his oneness with Life through the inner plane. Symbolically, when these four aspects of being are blended into the oneness of the Christ Mind, it will signify that mankind is ready for the ritual of placing the Apex Pyramidion on the great structure. This symbolizes the completion of the raising of the Feminine Ray.

The four men and the young woman reached the top and while they were making preparation for the simple ceremony, they could hear from the distant city of Cairo, some ten miles away, the chanting of the Moslem priests who, from early morning until sunrise, melodiously intone their mantram from their minarets high above the city. Dogs began to bark; an automobile horn could be heard afar off. One horn after another gave evidence of an awakening city. Soon the eastern sky was covered with gorgeous color and put on the finishing touches which tuned them in to a cosmic experience. (They all felt they were looking down the halls of history in ancient Mizraim.) The activity over the city seemed to recall the history of a land which in past ages had supported a highly developed civilization. They felt all that had gone on in the past, the majesty of the high culture of Atlantis. It seemed as though all records of the past history of that wonderful civilization were present again and right there with them. And they knew that these records must be transmuted by the fires of the resurrection flame that blazes in the etheric plane in the center of the Pyramid. For only by transmutation, the putting-off of the old man and the putting-on of the new, will humanity reach the apex of Being which is God, symbolized in the structure of the Great Pyramid.

On February 26, 1973, the ascension of Mark L. Prophet marked the fulfillment of the twelve-year cycle of the testimony of the two witnesses. His ascension climaxed the completion of the Piscean Age and the ushering-in of the Aquarian Age. Elizabeth Clare Prophet remains on earth to keep the Flame of the Mother, to hold the scepter of authority for the Church Universal and Triumphant. She is anointed by Jesus as the Vicar of Christ. The twin flames of Mark and Elizabeth, united with the Masters, focus the history of the cycle of the Great Pyramid both in the plane of Spirit and in the plane of Matter.

GOD'S WORD IN STONE — GOD'S WORD IN PRINT

Two Divinely Inspired Guides

For many years scholars have believed that certain verses in the Bible refer to a structure in the land of Egypt. They now are certain that it is the Great Pyramid of Gizeh.

When they began to accept this as a probability, it was not hard to see that many verses of the Old Testament prophets refer to the coming Golden Age when the chosen people or "the great innumerable multitude" make their final preparation to stand before the throne of God "arrayed in white robes," thus making it possible for the capstone to be placed on the Great Pyramid.

Adam Rutherford in his book on Pyramidology has defined the study of and significance of the Pyramid in these words: "Pyramidology is the science which coordinates, combines, and unifies science and religion, and is thus the meeting place for the two. When the

Great Pyramid is properly understood and universally studied, false religions and erroneous scientific theories alike will vanish. The true religion and the true science will be demonstrated to be harmonious.''

Thus man has two divinely inspired guides for God's plan for his evolvement: in stone and in print. The one in stone is the ancient wisdom scientifically exemplified in the Pyramid; the one in print is the ancient wisdom given in the Bible.

Built in Egypt

In that day shall there be an altar to the Lord in the midst of the land of Egypt, and a pillar at the border thereof to the Lord. And it shall be for a sign and for a witness unto the Lord of hosts in the land of Egypt: for they shall cry unto the Lord because of the oppressors, and he shall send them a saviour, and great one, and he shall deliver them. (Isa. 19:19, 20)

And the Lord answered me, and said, Write the vision, and make it plain upon tables, that he may run that readeth it. For the vision is yet for an appointed time, but at the end it shall speak, and not lie: though it tarry, wait for it; because it will surely come, it will not tarry. (Hab. 2:2, 3)

The Great, the Mighty God, the Lord of hosts, is his name . . . Which hast set signs and wonders in the land of Egypt. (Jer. 32: 18, 20)

Oh that my words were now written! Oh that they were printed in a book! That they were graven with an iron pen and lead in the rock for ever! (Job 19:23,24)

The rock has already stood in the desert for more than 125 centuries. In Job 19, verse 24, the word ''lead'' refers to the practice of filling carved inscriptions in stone with molten lead to protect the letters from the effects of the weather.

The Great Starry Universe

Many individuals among scholars and laymen are now willing to admit that the Pyramid was built by levitation; they are also willing to admit that the builders had an amazing understanding of astronomy, the great starry universe, and the planets. It is evident that the Lemurians and Atlanteans had knowledge of mathematics unheard of and beyond the understanding of present-day scientists.

There are many verses signifying knowledge of the stars by the inspired writers of the Bible.

When the morning stars sang together, and all the sons of God shouted for joy? (Job 38:7)

Canst thou bind the sweet influences of Pleiades, or loose the bands of Orion— (Job 38:31)

Which maketh Arcturus, Orion, and Pleiades, and the chambers of the south. (Job 9:9)

The Cornerstone

The Cornerstone of the Pyramid was itself a perfect pyramid in form — a crowning jewel of the entire structure. Both the Old and the New Testaments tell of the Apex Pyramidion that has been prepared, but was rejected by the builders due to the displacement in the construction of the Pyramid, and that it was used for the cornerstone. In Early Egyptian history any principal person was referred to as a corner stone.

The stone which the builders refused is become the head stone of the corner. This is the Lord's doing; it is marvellous in our eyes. (Ps. 118:22, 23)

Jesus saith unto them, Did ye never read in the scriptures, The stone which the builders rejected, the same is become the head of the corner: this is

the Lord's doing, and it is marvellous in our eyes?
(Matt. 21:42)

This is the stone which was set at nought of you
builders, which is become the head of the corner.
(Acts 4:11)

Jesus Christ himself being the chief corner stone.
(Eph. 2:20)

The stone which the builders disallowed, the same is
made the head of the corner, (I Pet. 2:7)

The Christ consciousness so well exemplified by
Jesus is the chief corner stone in every life.

The spiritual significance of displacement has been
discussed, and the rejection of the capstone by the
builders symbolizes the rejection of the Christ by
mankind.

The Casing Stones

The casing stones of the Pyramid were highly
polished white limestone curved slightly inward and
when the sun shone on them, it was said to have had the
appearance of a concave reflecting mirror. The stones
were marvellous for their size and accuracy, and people
who saw them in place said there was never another
building erected before or since to equal the Great
Pyramid for beauty and perfection.

Hast thou (Job) with him spread out the sky, which
is strong, and as a molten looking glass? (Job 37:18)

The Capstone

It is said that the capstone of the Pyramid will be put
in place when everyone has accepted his own personal
Christhood. Harmony will prevail and trouble and
human suffering will be at an end.

Students of the Bible believe that the passageways in the Pyramid tell God's plan for the spiritual progress of man through the millennium.

The wolf and the lamb shall feed together, and the lion shall eat straw like the bullock: and dust shall be the serpent's meat. They shall not hurt nor destroy in all my holy mountain, saith the Lord. (Isa. 65:25)

And he shall reign over the house of Jacob for ever; and of his kingdom there shall be no end. (Luke 1:33)

Violence shall no more be heard in thy land, wasting nor destruction within thy borders; but thou shalt call thy walls Salvation, and thy gates Praise . . . Thy people also shall be all righteous: they shall inherit the land for ever, the branch of my planting, the work of my hands, that I may be glorified. (Isa. 60:18, 21)

And there was given him dominion, and glory, and a kingdom, that all people, nations, and languages, should serve him: his dominion is an everlasting dominion, which shall not pass away, and his kingdom that which shall not be destroyed. (Dan. 7:14)

But they shall sit every man under his vine and under his fig tree; and none shall make them afraid: for the mouth of the Lord of hosts hath spoken it. (Mic. 4:4)

"The wolf also shall dwell with the lamb, and the leopard shall lie down with the kid; . . . and a little child shall lead them." (Isa. 11:6). This is to be the time when the capstone will be placed on the Pyramid indicating the beginning of the thousand year reign of the Christ.

We are approaching the golden age or millennium, the inauguration of which the Pyramid predicts for

1979. By this time the first three of the four groups of mankind will have completed their ceremony of circumambulation and can be designated as light-bearers.

The passing of the torch from the Piscean to the Aquarian Age through the Two Witnesses inaugurated the beginning of the cycle which brought the importance of the Mother Flame into prominence. This Flame had sunk with the continent of Lemuria and was kept submerged for its protection until such time as it could be accepted and begin its function to receive the Christ consciousness in a world of matter, so that the planet could begin its ascension spiral. It was brought to the heart center of The Summit Lighthouse at the time of the Ascension Class in April 1971 and left in charge of the Two Witnesses. The cycle man now enters could be known as the Resurrection of the Mother Flame, when humanity rises to the Christ consciousness and the Feminine Ray is being restored to its rightful place in both man and woman.

This period in pyramid history begins a new cycle known as the science of the Divine Mother which combines true science and religion for the bringing into manifestation of the perfectionment of God. It is the practical way to bring spirit into the plane of matter, thus raising the vibrations of all who dwell therein to the higher plane of knowledge.

Spirit and matter are really one substance but at different vibrational rates, matter being the denser. Only the power of the Feminine Ray or Mother consciousness is capable of raising these lower vibrations of matter into the higher plane of Christ consciousness.

Jesus was born into the plane of matter as are all mankind, but he so completely attained the Christ consciousness that he became the God-power. He put the capstone on his pyramid of life and fulfilled his mission. He came as the wayshower to give mankind the guide to the attainment of the Christ consciousness while yet in the plane of matter. As each individual lifestream masters the Christ consciousness and places the capstone on his pyramid of life, his displacement will be overcome.

MASTERS REFER TO THE PYRAMID

Excerpts from Masters' Dictations

In a dictation given by beloved Hercules at the Freedom Class, July 3, 1973, and published Jan. 27, 1974 in the **Pearls of Wisdom,** the following instruction was released.

"But Hierarchy has even greater admiration for souls on the Path who are raising their energies to the summit of being. To summon all that is in you, whether it be of darkness or whether it be of light, and to say 'Rise to the summit, the apex, and the crown!' demands the allness of your courage! For you know that when that energy reaches the crown, naught of the human consciousness shall remain! For all must be consumed in the capstone of the great Pyramid of Life.

"I desire to make you capstones in the Pyramid of Life and lively stones in the temple of being." (1 Pet. 2:5)

The following excerpt is from a dictation of beloved Lanello, given July 3, 1973 at the Freedom Class, and reprinted March 10, 1974 in **Pearls of Wisdom.**

"Those of you who are interested in history and who have a historical bent, those of you who are interested in archaeology, in the discoveries of the Pyramid, and those of you whose interest has not yet waxed hot — to you I say, there would be not one among you who would not be on the very edge of his seat in the chambers of the Brotherhood to see the true records of past history as these unfold and show clearly, written for all to see, that which is done in secret which is now shouted from the housetops (Luke 12:3), the very retreats of the Great White Brotherhood."

In his series of instructions on the Ascension given March 26 through July 30, 1967, in **Pearls of Wisdom,** beloved Serapis Bey makes the following references to the Pyramid.

"Thereby we shall be able to change the world into a place that will receive the masterful Presence of the living Christ in a second coming of such dimension as to produce a race of Godly men, of God-loving men, of God-fearing men — of men who will build a pyramid of Truth upon the plains of the world, which pyramid will stand the tests of erosion, of time, of mortal acidity and of human nonsense!" (Vol. X No. 22, May 28, 1967)

"Out of the depths of the infinite wisdom of God and from the heart of the Pyramid of Life, I have spoken. Let him who has an ear to hear, hear." (Vol. X No. 23, June 4, 1967)

"To this end must we work and serve. The pyramid of cosmic Truth, builded on lively stones, must rise on the great plains of Mamre. (Mam-Ray, symbolizing the Motherhood of God. See Gen. 18:1.) The eternal Mother must shield the eternal Son. The shell of cosmic purity must trumpet forth the victory of man in accordance with the divine plan." (Vol. X No. 31, July 30, 1967)

In Lesson 13 — Intermediate Studies of the Human Aura, November 24, 1974 beloved Djwal Kul informs us that "It is the square of the base of the pyramid that is built line upon line by the wise master builders who have learned to focus the threefold flame of the heart not only in the center of the pyramid, but also in the center of every stone that is laid according to the chief corner stone, the Christ consciousness without which no other stone is laid that is laid.''

During the Class of the Golden Cycle December 31, 1969 Lord Gautama released the Thoughtform for 1970. ''What do you think the Thoughtform for the year has become? A natural figure that some of you may have anticipated; for they say that coming events cast their shadows before them. In this case it is a Golden Pyramid with a white Capstone with the Eye of God looking every way within it; and the Light rays are magnificently pouring out from it. Your Pyramid Conference symbol, the symbol of the Great Seal of the United States, has now become a symbol of world building, of personal building, the building of the character of the individual, the building and raising of the Pyramid of Life, the elevation and construction of a new era as the decade begins; and all is centered in the magnificent Capstone of Life, Light and Love. The Eye of God, then, beholds the affairs of men, and whatsoever they do in secret shall be shouted from the housetops.''

The complete text of the dictation given by the Great Divine Director April 21, 1973 at the Class of the Ascension Flame and reprinted August 19 and 26, 1973 in **Pearls of Wisdom.**

A Replica of the Great Pyramid

Sons and Daughters of the Most High God:

Heaven salutes you in the hour of the vanquishment of human error. For though darkness increases as the rising tide of the consciousness of the mass mind expands the darkness from within, so the Light increases! The Light intensifies in the planetary body, in the heart of the earth, and in the hearts of the sons and daughters of the Infinite Fire.

I am come, the Initiator of Cycles! And in my right hand I bear a symbol, and the symbol is the replica of the Great Pyramid. And within that pyramid there is an ascending spiral of Light that cannot be denied its culmination in the capstone of Christ-reality made perfect in man as the power of the Logos. And why have I brought this symbol? Because I desire to make known to you that there shall be builded around the forcefield of your body temple by angelic hosts who serve the Initiator of Cycles the replica of the Great Pyramid.

For it is my desire — and I have expressed this desire before Almighty God — to create an experiment upon Terra to see if the children of the Light, and specifically the Keepers of the Flame, when given the opportunity of having within the forcefield of their consciousness the patterns of the Great Pyramid, will rise to the occasion and seize the opportunity to overcome and to be counted among the overcomers.

You see, it is one thing to know of the tests of the pyramid, of the king and queen's chamber and of the subterranean passage, the bottomless pit; it is another to experience that perfect balance of the Master Mason Himself. Stone upon stone, line upon line, the angels then begin to build the Great Pyramid around each one of you who will accept within your heart now this opportunity to be a living example of the overcoming of the tests of life.

I desire to see the side of the North perfected in **you!** Where else but in man and in woman can God appear? For this is the supreme creation of Life. I desire to see the side of the North, the memory body of each one of you, become as burnished steel, as fiery white Light, that the hand of Almighty God might descend to place its imprint upon the Book of Life within you. I desire to see the side of the East, the mental body of each one, become the pure golden yellow illumination of the Christ mind. And therefore I call forth the energies of Omega, of Alpha to arrest the spirals of the misuse of the active principle of the Godhead.

Legions now within these rooms, **burn** all that the Great Law will allow out of these devotees of the Flame! **Blaze** through them! And burn up the searing memories of human experience — all that can be taken that obstructs the divine memory. **Let** then the divine memory come forth, I say, of the Golden Ages and the origin of man. **Let** the divine ideations come forth in the mental body! Let the perfect geometric forms be established! For by the authority of my office and the power vested in me and the Light in the Cave of Light, I have come to challenge the warps in the mental belt. I have come to arrest the spirals of darkness and decay and death. Sheaths and layers are being withdrawn as though you were seated in the Cave of Light.

Angels of Light, now descend for the purification of the emotional quadrant! And let the Divine Mother appear within the heart, within the emotional body! And let the waters of the mind be still, be still by the power of the Elohim! **Ur!** [chant] I say, resist not; for angels of Love surround thee. **Blaze** the Light of Love into the feeling bodies and wash them clean! Wash them clean, wash them clean, wash them clean! **Burn** through and seize the serpentine lie! Angels of Light, build stone upon stone; and let the south side of the pyramid rise now.

I call to the Lords of Mind, Lords of Form, Lords of Individuality, and Lords of Creation to reestablish and align the atomic structure of the physical bodies of those assembled here. **Flow, O power** of the Holy Spirit! Let the will of God appear! Let the breath of the Holy Spirit

blow through, **blow** through, **blow** through the space between the foci of Light in man's body. So let the side of the West be the testimony of the Reality of God in manifestation.

Now then the inner workings of the Great Pyramid have focused within the power of the seven rays, the power of the secret rays, focuses of the chakras. Build on, angels of Light, noble creation. Thus the testing ground and the threshing floor of the Almighty has come within the forcefield of your consciousness. You have come to the mountain and the mountain has come to you. For this is the summit of attainment: to realize the power of the Eye of the Mind of God — and to place it upon the crown. My angels shall not place the capstone upon this pyramid. They shall instead allow you the privilege of doing so yourselves.

I said that I have made my desire known before God, pleading before His throne to make this experiment upon Terra. And if the experiment succeeds and a certain percentage among you rise to the level of the Christ Consciousness and remain there, holding the focus of the Great Pyramid for the nations, then more shall be given. But if the experiment fails and you do not honor the habitation of the Most High God, then that which you have shall be taken from you (Mark 4:25) and no more shall be added. Heaven is always ready to try — to try again and again and again, and to extend opportunity and hope to mankind. We are full of hope this night, for we have seen the devotion of your hearts. We are full of hope because we know what the Light of one heart in consummate abandon to the Flame of the Buddha can achieve for a planetary home.

Only one Light is needed, and yet many lights are here. What went ye out to see? A reed shaken by the wind? A pillar of fire? A cloud of witnesses? (Matt. 11:7;

Exod. 13:21; Heb. 12:1) Symbols in the air, now descend! Focus within these children of my heart the great symbols of the Sacred Fire from the ancient temples of Mu — symbols and hieroglyphs of Light that shall magnetize and demagnetize, magnetize and demagnetize, magnetize and demagnetize the Light, turning all darkness into Light, focusing the momentum of the Central Sun, the great houses of Reality and the Solar Hierarchies descending to defend, defending to descend, and so coming in the power of the Light, that mankind might ascend, that the planet earth might ascend, that elemental life might ascend!

This is the desire of the Almighty God this night, and this is the cycle that spirals through Cosmos at the velocity of the speed of Light, descending to penetrate your forcefields! For now you have been given those hieroglyphs of the priests of the Sacred Fire that shall focus within your consciousness, the **power** of the Great Divine Director, the wisdom of the Great Divine Director, the love of the Great Divine Director to release to the mankind of earth the full-gathered momentum of the resurrection spiral that shall not leave mankind as he was found, but raise him to the heights of Christ-mastery and the ascension spiral that is the goal of Life for every man!

Know you now what has transpired? You have been placed for that brief moment in an acceleration chamber made possible by the forcefield of the Great Pyramid upon your consciousness, a chamber that can accelerate the velocity and intensity of Life within you preparatory for your own ascension. And the very atoms of your being during that moment were stepped up, that they might have the impression upon the memory bank and the memory body of what it is like to be raised by the fires of the ascension current to that point of the apex of the Pyramid that is the ascended Jesus Christ Consciousness for all mankind.

O beloved mankind, how Saint Germain desires to step through the veil, to place a focus of the ascension chair within your midst, to give you the opportunity within an outer retreat of the Great White Brotherhood such as this to make progress steadfast in the Light! How Heaven waits, hoping that enough devotees will purify and rectify and make whole, that Heaven might lower into manifestation greater and greater dispensations of Light!

But ah, how the karmic cycles have woven an intensity of self-destruction upon mankind so that if we were to increase our focuses of Light, it would be a matter of mankind's own self-destruction when they approached our focuses! And therefore out of love for humanity, we have tempered the wind of the Holy Spirit to the shorn lamb of mankind's identity — but not for long.

For I perceive upon the hillsides of the world devotees clothed in white, saints robed in holy attire, moving in the spirals, swaying in the symphony of the air to the worship of the Mother Flame. And there where the elect are gathered together (Matt. 24:28, 31), there will the mighty eagle of the Great God Star Sirius descend as the formation of angels of white fire and blue lightning, legions to descend and hold consort with the saints upon the hillsides of the world.

Harmony is the requirement. Precious hearts, know you not that when you are disturbed, no matter what the cause — of world conditions, inner turmoil — you cannot hold consort with the heavenly hosts. I am asking you to surrender within your heart and the spirals of disturbance concerning the rightness and the wrongness of actions in the world, in the family, in the community. Rightness and wrongness are but phases of the human consciousness. Do you not understand this? There is only Reality and unreality. Within unreality there is the entire spectrum of mankind's justices and injustices. Forsake them all! Be free of the inner strife! Be free of the alignment of your consciousness to the stars of the world, figureheads, personalities, warring factions.

For I have come to set you free from all that — from all the struggles of the world and the sense of struggle. For I would raise you to the heights of Christ-mastery, that you might stand and pronounce the great word of "peace!" to command the waves to be still (Mark 4:39), command the fires to take the form of the Christ, command the earth to be molded in the image of the Holy Spirit.

Sit no longer in the seat of the scornful (Pss. 1:1), in condemnation, in self-righteousness; but withdraw to the center of Being. And there within the sheaths of the secret rays you will find the protection that is the perfection of the Light. Go within and find the ray of the Mother. And when you go within, all initiations that come to you will be passed successfully because you are protected by the sheaths of the secret rays.

No problems of the world can be solved by the outer consciousness, but only by going within. But going within is not to lie down and be trampled upon by the hooves of horses that gallop in the night. Going within is to affirm the Be-ness of God that has all power to align all conditions in the world at large.

And now the angels have completed the inner chambers and the focuses of the great chakras. This forcefield will rest upon you for a twelve-month cycle. If it is used, amplified by you, it will be renewed again automatically at the end of the twelve months. If it is neglected, it will be withdrawn. Within that twelve-month cycle, you will experience the test of the ten and the initiations of the Twelve Solar Hierarchies within the Pyramid of Life. Three in one, three in one, three in one, three in one!

And so the pilgrimage that you desired to make to the Great Pyramid, to all of its chambers, is fulfilled in you this night. How blessed is the Lord God! How loving! How great his concern for each one of you! Our love is boundless; and if you knew the great love of the angelic hosts and the masters for each one of you, I am certain that your efforts would be increased a thousandfold. And therefore, for a moment within these walls, our legions will intensify the action of love from the throne of your Divinity. [Pause]

Intensify! Immensify! Magnify! O Love of God, press upon the hearts of these ones! Melt the darkness! Melt the hardness! Melt the recalcitrance and the impositions of the world! O Love, set their hearts aglow! Set them afire! [Pause]

At the conclusion of this dictation, the action of Love sustained by your own Heart Flame will resume the normal frequency. But you will not be the same, for the very cells of your heart are impressed with the memory of God's love. And so the pattern has been set for you to magnetize that great love again. I have initiated a love spiral within you, but you must fulfill that spiral — if you wish. For God will not impose Himself upon you, precious hearts; for He desires that you come because you love, because you have free will.

Hear then, precious children. Do you sometimes feel that the Ascended Masters come as Santa Claus to bestow the many gifts of the Sacred Fire from the pack upon their backs? Well, you know, we enjoy playing the role of Santa Claus; and we carry that mighty pink flame of love that was within the heart of Saint Nicholas.

Precious hearts, as we focus our consciousness in the All-Seeing Eye of God and behold the great manifestations of His great glow-ray, we are transfigured again and again. And there are cycles of transfiguration that transcend each other; and so through the initiations of hierarchy, the thirty-three steps are repeated over and over and over again, and the Cosmos is ever new. And it is out of the grand perspective of the divine order of life that we find the fulfillment of the will of God. As above, so below. In this perspective we perceive no problem too hard for the Lord.

We transcend cycles; we cut across cycles, lines of force where all is God and there is none else beside Him. We enter other orbits, other galaxies, where error is no more and the Light does shine.

And from far-off worlds
We know that the fulcrum
Of the power of the universe
Is sufficient to thrust
The very dust of the earth
Into the Flame
And bring mankind to her feet again
Before the Almighty One
Who is indeed a blazing Sun.
Dazzling, golden-pink glow-ray,
Is the Light, the Fire, I say,
Reaching the farthest edges of space
Where there is a mirror,
And in that mirror behold the face
Of Christed ones ascending.

And so the great story unending
Of man perfecting, being perfected,
Is come, is come again.
And there in the far reaches,

I AM the consciousness of the Initiator of Cycles.
There is a heightening,
A glorying effect
Of Light mirrored in Light,
Love reflected in Truth,
Truth reflected in Love.
How the starry fires of the universe
Beam the Light waves of attainment
Across the skies!
And mankind's consciousness, as it expands,
Is intercepted by interplanetary bands
Forcefields of Ascended Ones
Who have accepted their role in life
To be electrodes of Mighty Power,
Mighty Love, Mighty Wisdom.

Take dominion then, I say,
Sons and daughters of Mary —
Of the Mother Ray!
Take dominion in the footstool kingdom!
Take that kingdom and fling it into the Flame
To do His will in God's own name!
For it is the will to do
And the doing of the will
That shall return this orb
Into the starry height
To be a testimony throughout eternity
Of the overcomers who have won the fight!

The Karmic Board salutes you and by the power of
the seven rays charges you to be representatives of God-
justice upon the earth.

Courage, O hearts of fire!
Courage, I say!
For the Light of the New Day shall dawn!
And you shall win all the way!

GLOSSARY

Cartouche of Cheops: The hallmark of Khufu, 4th dynasty, was placed on stones from the royal quarries. These marks have been found on parts of the Great Pyramid and presented as proof that it was built during his reign. In view of other information this seems to be very meager evidence. It is most likely that he simply restored portions damaged by intruders, as certain stelas in the area tell of repairs he made on the Sphinx.

Great Seal of the United States: The Pyramid without a headstone found on the reverse of the Great Seal becomes more and more significant in a study of the Great Pyramid. Along its base is MDCCLXXVI (1776) and above it is suspended the Apex Pyramidion against a blaze of light ready to be placed when the United States has fulfilled her spiritual mission. Within the triangle is an open eye and above it the words Annuit Coeptis, "God has favored our undertaking," which alludes to the many signal directions of providence in favor of the country's cause. Across a banner bordering the lowest half is Novus Ordo Seclorum, "A New Order of the Ages."

Immortelles: During the Easter Conference in 1971, beloved Omega made La Tourelle a focal point for the resurrection spiral and gave authority to immortalize cut flowers. Since that time, many flowers have been immortalized. The color of the blossom remains, and the leaves and petals do not fall off.

One may see bouquets and floral arrangments of these lovely flowers throughout the heart center, and many members have taken these arrangements home with them, as a spiral of the resurrection flame is anchored in each one for a healing focus.

Teleois Numerology: A system of proportions used as a sacred code by ancient wise men to communicate knowledge from one civilization to another. This mysterious series of numbers and proportions is found in musical scales, designs of snowflakes and in every beautiful structure in Greek art. It also determines the structure of all key temples in Palestine, Tibet, Ancient Cathay, Mayaland, and Eastern Andes. The width and length of each comet path is in Teleois proportions. After 38 years of research it was rediscovered in 1898.

BIBLIOGRAPHY

Benavides, Rodolfo, **Dramatic Prophecies of The Great Pyramid,** Mexico, D.F. Translation of the eleventh edition which appeared in Mexico 1970. The facts concerning the Great Pyramid are reviewed and studied from both the scientific and esoteric point of view.

Bullinger, W.W., **Number in Scripture.** London: The Lamp Press Ltd., 1952. The relationship of numbers to the works and Word of God makes thrilling reading for the layman. The spiritual significance of the numbers is invaluable to the serious student of the Bible.

Cayce, Edgar Evans, **Edgar Cayce on Atlantis.** New York: Hawthorne Books, Inc., 1968. The existence of Atlantis verified by life readings which revealed the experiences of individuals who had been Atlanteans.

Davidson, David, **The Great Pyramid, Its Divine Message.** Reprinted. David Davidson, Leeds, England, a structural engineer of great ability, became interested in the construction of the Pyramid. He set out to prove the fallacy of its divine origin and its prophetic revelation. Instead he established mathematically and proved to his own satisfaction that the Pyramid is divine by construction and number revelation. This monumental work is couched in technical terms of a mathematician-scientist and is difficult for the layman to read. It, nevertheless, is a major contribution to the knowledge and understanding of the Great Pyramid. Illustrated.

Davidson, David, **Miracles of History.** London: The Covenant Publishing Company, Ltd., 1947. A collection of previously published articles relating to events of history from the Exodus to the middle of the 20th century and their confirmation in Pyramid measurements. Its purpose is to inform and incite in the reader the need for individual and national preparation for the fulfillment of the prophecies.

Flanagan, G. Pat, **The Pyramid and Its Relationship to Bio-Cosmic Energy.** 1972. The author has taken bio-cosmic energy out of "opinion entwined in religious and occult practices" and placed it in the realm of science with some exciting results. In fact, a whole new field of science is evolving out of this research wherein a structure shape of the Great Pyramid is found to be a powerful source of bio-cosmic energy.

Flanagan, G. Pat, **Pyramid Power.** Glendale, Calif. Pyramid Publishers, 1974. A review of ancient knowledge of Life Energy introduces a comprehensive discussion of the mathematics of The Great Pyramid of Gizeh and the factors relating to pyramid phenomena.

Landone, Brown, **Prophecies of Melchi-Zedek** in the Great Pyramid and the Seven Temples. New York: The Book of Gold, 1940. Valuable information concerning Teleois Numerology as it relates to the Pyramid, and calls attention to other temples of the world which have the same proportionate measurements.

Nicklin, J. Bernard, **Testimony in Stone.** Merrimac, Mass. Destiny Publishers, 1961. A comprehensive, factual presentation that demonstrates the synchronization of Bible prophecies and Pyramid number revelations.

Prophet, Mark and Elizabeth, **Climb the Highest Mountain,** Book 1, The Summit Lighthouse, Colorado Springs, Colorado, 1972. The first of five volumes comprising a treatise on cosmic law for the two-thousand-year cycle that marks the Aquarian Age, the golden age of freedom and the expansion of soul consciousness through peace and enlightenment.

Rand, Howard B., **The Challenge of the Great Pyramid.** Merrimac, Mass. Destiny Publishers, 1966. (Out of Print.) A concise and authoritative account of the cosmic science and Bible prophecy built into this ancient symbol. Illustrated.

Robinson, Lytle W., **The Great Pyramid and Its Builders.** Virginia Beach, Va. Association of Research and Enlightenment, Fifth Printing, 1967. Six hundred of the Edgar Cayce readings were studied that this history of the builders of the Pyramid might be compiled. It was revealed to Edgar Cayce that he, as the Priest Ra, planned the structure and Hermes, a descendent of Hermes Trismegistus, worked out the details of construction.

Rutherford, Adam, **Pyramidology,** in five volumes. Institute of Pyramidology, 31 Station Road, Harpenden, Hertfordshire, Great Britain.

   Book I — **Elements of Pyramidology,** revealing the divine plan for our planet.
   Book II — **Christ Revealed by the Pyramid.**
   Book III — **Coordination of Great Pyramid Chronograph, Bible Chronology and Archaeology.**
   Book IV — **History of the Great Pyramid.**
   Book V — **The Revelation of Science in the Pyramid** (in preparation)

Tompkins, Peter, **Secrets of the Great Pyramid,** New York, N.Y. Harper and Row, 1971. A comprehensive study with many facets of pyramidology as it pertains to the Great Pyramid. Credit is given to the many men through the years who have contributed revelations of the Pyramid and their work reviewed and compared. Profusely illustrated with select pictures and drawings.

For information on
The Summit Lighthouse
Church Universal and Triumphant
and conferences and seminars
conducted by
Elizabeth Clare Prophet
write to:
Box A
Colorado Springs
Colorado 80901
or contact any
of the following centers:

Church Universal and Triumphant
International Headquarters
Summit University
Montessori International
1539 East Howard Street
Pasadena, CA 91104

Church Universal and Triumphant
Retreat of the Resurrection Spiral
First and Broadmoor
Colorado Springs, CO 80906

Church Universal and Triumphant
Keepers of the Flame Motherhouse
2112 Santa Barbara Street
Santa Barbara, CA 93105

Church Universal and Triumphant
Los Angeles Community Teaching Center
1130 Arlington Avenue
Los Angeles, CA 90019

Church Universal and Triumphant
San Francisco Community Teaching Center
P.O. Box 27463
San Francisco, CA 94127

Church Universal and Triumphant
Boulder Community Teaching Center
P.O. Box 3571
Boulder, CO 80303

Church Universal and Triumphant
Minneapolis/St. Paul Community Teaching Center
1206 Fifth Street SE
Minneapolis, MN 55414

Church Universal and Triumphant
New York City Community Teaching Center
P.O. Box 667
Lenox Hill Station
New York, NY 10021

Church Universal and Triumphant
Washington, D.C. Community Teaching Center
4715 Sixteenth Street NW
Washington, D.C. 20011

You are invited
to study the teachings
of the Ascended Masters
published by The Summit Lighthouse
as Pearls of Wisdom
and sent to you
on a love-offering basis.
For information
write to:
The Summit Lighthouse
Box A
Colorado Springs
Colorado 80901

For information
on Summit University
write to:
Summit University
Box A
Colorado Springs
Colorado 80901